GOD'S BUSINESS PARTNER, PROPHETIC QUESTION, AND SPECIAL PRAYERS

Jenness Reid

www.worksoftrinity.com

Published by Works Of Trinity, LLC
Teaneck, New Jersey, 07666, U.S.A.
www.worksoftrinity.com

All scripture quotations are taken from The Holy Bible, King James Version (KJV) – *public domain.*

No part of this book may be reproduced, or stored in a retrieval system, or transmitted in any form or by any means, electronic, mechanical, photocopying, recording, or otherwise, without express written permission of the publisher.

Email: permission@worksoftrinity.com.

God's Business Partner, Prophetic Question, And Special Prayers

Copyright © 2021 Jenness Reid, all rights reserved.

ISBN-13: 978-0-9831999-8-4 (paperback)
ISBN-13: 978-0-9831999-9-1 (electronic)

Cover design by: Jenness Reid
Printed in the United States of America

DEDICATION

I dedicate this book to the works of The Trinity. This is my vision of God's children doing His works on earth through the power of God, Jesus Christ of Nazareth, and The Holy Spirit. This book is written by request of The Holy Spirit.

Contents

Acknowledgements i
Who Requested This Book? 1
I Need Help!!! 6
Insights into the Works of God 11
God Prayed for Amazon 19
Reshaping the World through Prayer 25
I Need More Help 50
This Is It. Really? 55
Redirected to Victory 58
A Leader's Prayer for Change, in a Time of Crisis 74
The Question of Social Change 87
Get Noticed 100
Bibliography 103
About the Author 105
Books By This Author 106

Acknowledgements

First, I give thanks to God for directing my path in all that I do for Him. May this book and all that I do bring Him glory. He led me to re-title this book to specify more of its content.

Who Requested This Book?

Do you know of any company that has a story which falls into the category of, "Divine Intervention?" If so, let it be heard. The works of God should not be kept hidden. He is worthy to be praised, glorified, and acknowledged in every area of our lives, even in the corporate world.

Whatever your story might be, mine is unique. The writing of this book is under the direction of The Holy Spirit of God – our Creator. He has a story to tell – the story of putting together His team of business partners in which Amazon plays a central role.

I have written three books about my experiences with God, Jesus Christ of Nazareth, and The Holy Spirit of God. All of my experiences could not be contained in these books. There are a lot more to be told, and this bit about Amazon is just a small part of the rest. The books that caused a partnership to be formed with Amazon were written under the guidance of Jesus Christ. They are: *God Works Through Dreams, God's Mission: Spiritual Battles And Revelation of Anti-666,* and *God Has Gone Corporate.*

Who Requested This Book?

From a very young age, I have been a book reader, but never an author. But then, the challenge came. Jesus Christ of Nazareth requested that I write books for Him about the many experiences I have been through. Accepting the challenge, but not knowing what to do, Jesus Christ lined up business partners to help me along the way. This book is mainly focused on the crucial help I got from Amazon along the way and the prayer that changed Amazon to be the Amazon we now know.

The partnership with Amazon was not straightforward. There were other paths taken along the way, but God knew who He wanted to partner with to establish His company. This book gives the reader an insight into how God conducts His business.

Please do not expect to see any logic in how God does His works, or what God uses to do His work, or who God uses to do His work. He does not operate according to worldly standards. He uses what the world considers to be foolish things to shame the wise and the weak things to shame the strong. The foolishness of God is wiser than that of mankind and the weakness of God is stronger than that of mankind (1 Corinthians 1:20-25).

Many of those who God calls are not wise, powerful, or of noble birth, according to worldly standards. However, God chooses the low and despised in the world, even things that seem insignificant to bring down things that seem significant. He does this to humble us and for us to give Him the glory (1 Corinthians 1:26-29).

I Need Help!!!

Now that I say, "Yes" to Jesus Christ to not only write books about my experiences, but to publish them myself, what do I do? The thought of publishing books was very daunting, but I trusted Jesus Christ and was determined to do His will – His will for me to write books and self-publish them.

From 2011, I started to check out book publishers and read about book publishing. At the same time, I continued to write manuscripts for three books, in parallel.

It was good that I own the stories and therefore did not have to worry about having contents. However, the more I read about book publishing, the more I realized that I needed help and lots of it. I knew that not self-publishing would cause God's plan to fall apart. But, what do I do?

I felt like I was in serious trouble with my book writing and publishing assignment. I called on the One Who gave me this assignment to help and deliver me, so that He can get the glory (Psalms 50:15). I have read many books and saw many styles of writing, but how do I measure up to the standard required of publishers?

I Need Help!!!

I felt the guidance of The Holy Spirit as I researched book printing services. Knowing for Whom I was doing this work gave me the zeal to carry on and to do my very best.

What I had to do was by far no easy task. I needed a business partner, but which one? God did not immediately expose me to Amazon. He wanted me to compare what others had to offer; otherwise, I would not appreciate what He had in store for me. I came across book printers that required having books in stock for order fulfillment, charged setup fees, and had per volume processing fees. I really did not have the kind of money it would take to even start with such options. I continued to pray and search.

I came across CreateSpace – an Amazon

subsidiary. They allowed self-publishing. I liked what they were offering – free setup, cover and interior templates, specifications for book cover and book interior, and book distribution. For interior and book cover, they offered a lot of "how to" do each task in the process of writing, uploading, and reviewing. They also had information on advertising books.

I understood that book sales from CreateSpace would be online through Amazon. However, at the time, I was not clear on how my books would be made available to brick-and-mortar stores. In 2013, I did basic signed up since this was the best route I came across.

I was used to buying books in bookstores, so my preference was to have my books readily available in bookstores. As such, I continued my search for a book printing partner. In my search, I came across a book printing company which offered similar printing services as CreateSpace, but for small fees. I liked their direct sales to brick-and-mortar bookstores. My preference was to have my books sitting on the shelf, waiting for buyers. Sad to say, I do not know what the future holds; only God does.

Insights into the Works of God

Are you able to recognize the works of God in your life, or in your business? Sometimes people mistake the movement of God in their lives to be coincidence, their own thinking, or their own innovation. The works of God is accomplished by His Holy Spirit working through individuals who allow this and through any of His vast creation.

Insights into the Works of God

To better understand when God is working in your life, it is necessary to know something about the gifts of the Spirit of God to His children. Therefore, before talking about some extremely powerful prayers, prayed by The Holy Spirit of God, through me, I will write briefly about the gifts of The Holy Spirit of God.

In Corinthians 12, the Apostle Paul listed nine gifts of The Holy Spirit of God. The gifts are diverse, but operated by the same Spirit. Children of God are given gifts of the Spirit to benefit everyone.

The children of God might have one or more of the gifts of the Spirit. The available gifts are – the word of wisdom, the word of knowledge, faith, healing, working of miracles, prophecy, discerning of spirits, different kinds of tongues (unknown language to the speaker), and interpretation of tongues.

According to Prince (2007), the gifts of the Spirit are all supernatural. We cannot explain any of them "by natural talent, education, or ability. A word of wisdom or knowledge is not the kind of wisdom or knowledge that comes from spending fifteen years in college" (p. 9). Word of wisdom or knowledge is given by The Holy Spirit.

The gift of the Spirit is further categorized into groups of three – revelation gifts (a word of wisdom, a word of knowledge, and discerning of spirits), power gifts (faith, gifts of healings, and workings of miracles), and vocal gifts (different kinds of tongues, interpretation of tongues, and prophecy).

You cannot earn Spiritual gifts; you can only receive them. They are for useful, practical, and profitable purposes. When a child of God has The Holy Spirit on the inside, the things that He does within that child are manifestations of His presence. He will do things in specific ways.

The movement of The Holy Spirit can be compared to the wind which blows wherever it pleases. You hear it, but cannot tell where it comes from or goes (John 3:8). This wind comparison will come in handy for you to understand some of what I will described later about the movement of The Holy Spirit.

An outstanding Biblical story about movement of The Holy Spirit is found in Act chapter 2. Acts 2:1-4 describes what happened on the day of Pentecost when The Holy Spirit descended from heaven to dwell within members of the newly formed church of Jesus Christ on earth (Prince, 2007). The Holy Spirit came suddenly from heaven, like a rushing mighty wind and filled the house. They could see the Holy Spirit in the form of divided tongues that looked like fire, sitting on each of the church member. The Holy Spirit then caused them to speak in other tongues (languages not known to them).

The manifestation of The Holy Spirit from within these church members caused about three thousand people to surrender to Jesus Christ (Act 2:41). Sound is a manifestation of The Holy Spirit, which can be recognized through the sense of hearing. Maybe someone present can interpret the language or sound coming from the individual, under the power of The Holy Spirit.

Children of God are to demonstrate the power of the Holy Spirit through the supernatural gift stated in 1 Corinthians 12. The faith of God's children "should not be based on intellectual or philosophical arguments, or on seminary training and degrees… but on the personal experience of God's power" (Prince, 2007, p.46).

I have many experiences with The Holy Spirit; at times He gives me immediate knowledge when exposed to a situation. When I recognize the works of God in the situation, I call it a "spiritual incident." Spiritual incidents can connect things and/or circumstances together to form a solution.

Insights into the Works of God

Some people refer to "spiritual incident" as "coincident." However, when you can clearly see the works of God in the situation, you will know it is a "spiritual incident." For example, you can pray about a problem and later come across the solution, suddenly and in an unexpected way. You can have sudden inspirational thoughts. You can suddenly connect to what someone is saying, or doing. You can suddenly notice something that you have passed by many times before, without noticing. Movements of The Holy Spirit often have a "sudden" or "unexpected" element to them.

The Holy Spirit of God is not limited in the ways He works through God's children who give Him the freedom to work through them. Spiritual incidents, under the power of The Holy Spirit, not only happen to individuals, but also in businesses.

A lot more can be said about the gifts and movements of The Holy Spirit; however, this is just a little insight into the workings of The Holy Spirit to prepare the reader to better understand some of the stories in later chapters. To learn more about the gifts of The Holy Spirit, I recommend reading the book by Derek Prince, listed in the bibliography.

God Prayed for Amazon

In 2014, without consulting The Holy Spirit, I also signed up with the other printing company which distributes books to brick-and-motor bookstores. Instead of one contract, I had to sign three; they had separate contracts for Apple and Amazon. I did not like the idea of having to sign separate contracts for Apple and Amazon.

About the same time of the contracts signing, I heard of a book which The Holy Spirit indicated I should purchase. Its title is, "*Digital Disruption: Unleashing the Next Wave of Innovation*" by James McQuivey. I searched the internet to get the best price for this book. When I saw that the price on Amazon was about ten dollars less than a popular bookstore, I was concerned. I did not understand that this was the author's marketing strategy. I was wondering why the price was not consistent and how things would work with my books.

That night, I woke up with a slight headache and was wondering why. I knew I was still concerned about selling books on Amazon. However, God knew there was no need to be concerned. I suddenly felt that I should pray.

I knelt beside my bed. I started to pray,

"Heavenly Father, you know that I am concerned about the Amazon contract." The Holy Spirit responded by asking me to give Him the books. I said, "Heavenly Father, I give you the books."

The Holy Spirit went into action immediately. He took over my prayer and started to pray, through me, and in a language which I did not understand. Christians commonly refer to this as "praying in tongues."

I knew The Holy Spirit was praying about the books because He had me using my hands, in prophetic movements. I was rubbing one against the other in fists and then flat; The Holy Spirit then allowed me to have my palms together as I made cutting motions in various directions, in front of me and to the sides of me. He then allowed me to place my hands side by side, palms up, as how you would open a book to read. Next, I raised my hands to my face, as if reading. I stayed in this position for a while as The Holy Spirit continued to pray, through me and in a language I did not understand.

At times, I would mention Amazon. I declared that God is in control and He is mighty. After about 10 minutes, The Holy Spirit released me from executing His works.

God certainly moved swiftly to put me at ease with Amazon. After all, He knows the future and everything is under His control. After the prayer, I felt better about my book sales on Amazon.

The way The Holy Spirit used me to

execute the answer to the pray while He was praying, through me, was not strange to me. It does not happen all the time, but I have experienced it before. I could see what I was doing in the physical, but I had no idea how God was dealing with the prayer His Holy Spirit was praying.

What was the result of The Holy Spirit's prayer for Amazon? I did not know what to expect. I only knew that it had something to do with my books. What I observed is that, about six months later, I started to see what I recognized as the impact of this prayer on Amazon. The prosperity of Amazon had begun. It started with them getting airplanes to help in their package delivery. From that point onwards, I continuously hear of one innovation after the other coming from Amazon; without a doubt, bringing challenges, opportunities, and sometimes fear to the business community.

I soon realized that the prayer The Holy Spirit had prayed for Amazon was one to prosper the company. God positioned His business partner, so that they can, in term, help to establish His business. I did not understand it all at first. The works of God is not readily understood; even by those who are close to Him.

Reshaping the World through Prayer

I mentioned in the previous chapter that the way The Holy Spirit used me to execute His prayer for Amazon was not strange to me. It is worthwhile giving other examples of The Holy Spirit's prayers which, I think, will astound readers.

Before going further into more prayer examples by The Holy Spirit, let's take a look at what E.M. Bound said in his book, *E.M. Bound on PRAYER,* about prayer and the works of God on earth. He said that it is the prayer of God's children that is used in heaven to carry out great works of God, on earth; that prayer causes earth to change, to be revolutionized; that angels move more quickly and with greater power because of prayer; and that prayer shapes God's policy when the prayers of His children are more numerous and more efficient (Bound, 1920).

If prayer has greater power based on more of God's children praying, what then can we say of prayer from The Holy Spirit of God, to God Himself? I hope you are ready to hear more about prayers by The Holy Spirit of God.

Before going further, let me say a little

about my background, as a Christian. Growing up, I was rooted in the Presbyterian Church. At a very young age, around four years old, I could feel the presence of The Holy Spirit whenever Reverend DeCasta preached. After he left the church, while I was still very young, it was as if the presence of The Holy Spirit left with him.

There is a huge gap between my experience with The Holy Spirit as a child and as an adult. As a matter of fact, I did not know that the enlightening feeling I was getting when hearing Reverend DeCasta preached was from The Holy Spirit. I only recognized that now.

My experiences with The Holy Spirit grew rapidly after going through some unexpected and shocking spiritual warfare. I wrote about these experiences in my other books. After I started going to a Holy Spirit-filled church, I learned more about prayer and movements of The Holy Spirit. I had an experience with my very first Daniel fast, which is worth mentioning.

I did my first Daniel fast with two prayer partners. In that fast, I focused on praying for God to take back His glory in the earth. On the last day of the 21-days fast, while praying with my prayer partners, The Holy Spirit spoke out, through me, that "something big, big…, happened in heaven." I could not stop myself from repeating the word "big" continuously for about 5 minutes, before I could finish the sentence. After this, The Holy Spirit spoke that, "The army of Heaven is activated."

What does that mean? I am not sure. I only know that my heart for God is for Him to get the glory He deserves, on this earth – His creation.

In writing this book, I realize that The Holy Spirit of God wants to share quite a few of His prayers for the reader to get a better understanding of Him. God uses me in prayer in many different ways. One unknown prayer story is about The Holy Spirit calling on me to pray for President Obama, on multiple occasions. At least twice, The Holy Spirit woke me up to pray for President Obama.

Whenever I started to pray, The Holy Spirit would take over and have me praying like a soldier, fighting a war. On each prayer occasion, I would hear the next day of a security incident at the White House. Each time, the perpetrator would be caught. President Obama made it safely out of the White House because God was protecting him.

I took you through two prayer examples to prepare you for the next one. But, are you really prepared for it? In December of 2017, my prayer partners and I had outstanding experiences, which show that God is reshaping the world, through prayer. It happened on a Norwegian cruise. I went on the cruise with my sister, Ruth, her friend, Petra, and Petra's family.

Ruth and I shared a room at the bow of the ship. On Sunday, Petra came to our room and we had church service there. We sang a few praise songs. Ruth and Petra prayed and then I joined them in prayer. At one point, the Holy Spirit started praying, through me, mostly in tongues (a language I was not able to understand).

I spoke a few words in English. I was telling God to take back His glory. I was saying that everyone is "out of order." I was declaring "order," continuously for a few minutes. While praying, I was making prophetic moves with strong movements, which I could feel throughout my body. My hands were first outstretched, horizontally; later, I had them up in the air. After a while, I started pulling down, strongly, with up and down movements of my right hand. After a while, I started clapping both hands together, palm together in a praying format, as I pushed them in front of me.

I moved around slowly, while declaring the word, "order." After a while, both Petra and Ruth joined me in clapping their hands together, as I declared, "order."

Although I knew I was praying about the glory of God to be returned to earth, I could not interpret what The Holy Spirit was praying. After the prayer was over, Petra repeatedly said, "Oh my God, Oh my God." When she was able to control herself, she told us that something so awesome happened. She said that the gift of interpretation of tongues had manifested in her before, but she had never interpreted an intercessory prayer, prayed in tongues.

Petra had been praying for a new revelation of the Lord and an opportunity to witness to others, while on the cruise. The Lord gave her the revelation of interpreting and understanding The Holy Spirit's prayer. She understood, for the first time, the magnitude, depth, and power of The Holy Spirit's prayer. She said the prayer, in tongues, had great power.

Petra did not remember the prayer word-for-word, so she paraphrased what she remembered when relating it to us. The Holy Spirit began by proclaiming who God was.

"My God, You are mighty! You are powerful! You are majestic! You are vast! There is no measure to You, no height, nor depth, nor width. You are bigger than the world and the entire universe. You stretch past the heavens and the earth. Your power cannot be understood by men.

Your enormity and eternal nature cannot be fully grasped by those You created. Your worth is incomprehensible to Your people. From everlasting to everlasting You exist; You create and You sustain. How mighty! How powerful! How vast! None can describe Who You are, none can express Your nature and power in fullness. I give You the full glory You deserve, the honor and praise. I bow before You my God and King and I bless You according to Who You are and all that You do."

Petra mentioned that somehow the language of the tongues magnified the proclamations a million times more than the words of the prayer she recorded. She remembered understanding with these words, but understood so much more in her spirit than the earthly words are conveying.

The Holy Spirit continued to praise and magnify the Lord in a way Petra had heard no man praise God. It was as if, because our knowledge and understanding of Who God is, is limited, our praise which is according to our understanding, is also limited. But The Holy Spirit knows Who God is in fullness and is able to ascribe to Him all the praise and glory and honor He deserves, in Spirit and in Truth.

The prayer of The Holy Spirit continued; *"My God, in the olden days, Your people knew You. They understood You. They worshipped You out of a full knowledge of Who You are and what You have done. They understood that everything they were and had, came from You. Everything around, above and below them, came from You. You were everything, they knew it. They praised You with pure hearts, in Spirit and in Truth. There was nothing holding them back, nothing dampening, or contaminating, or limiting their praises. There was no deception, no pretense, no lack of knowledge of Who You are, no materialism. It was man and God, one on one."*

Petra saw a vision of what looked like tribal people of old; face down on the ground worshipping God, as if they could not stand in His Holy presence but reverenced Him so much that they lay prostrate on the dirt, in awe, gratefulness, and worship.

The prayer of The Holy Spirit continued; *"But now my God, look at the world You created.*

Look at the people You created. They have forgotten Who You are. They have turned away from the truth. They have locked away the praise that belongs to You in their hearts.

Your glory is everywhere but they can no longer see. They are blinded by deception, pretense, ambition, and pride. They ignore You and refuse to praise You. The praise is Yours, my God. It belongs to You. You created them to praise You. You created them with praise in their hearts.

My God, reach out and pluck their hearts of stone out and give them hearts that will praise You. Reach out and release the praise from their hearts. My God, do something! Fix it! Fix it Lord. Strip away the barriers between You and Your people. Break down the walls of deception and lies. You can fix this my God. Bring Your people back to when they knew You and understood Who You are; when they comprehended Your power and might.

My God extract the praise from their hearts. Let all of creation praise and worship You again, as You deserve. Let Your praises rise from the earth like never before."

Petra saw the Lord laying down the world as if it was a map on the ground and the countries as puzzle pieces in the world map. There were pieces out of place and God was fixing them. He was putting the countries back in order; the world back in order, spiritually; not just the lands, but the people who were so far away from God and refusing to give Him the glory due unto Him.

The prayer of The Holy Spirit continued;

"My God, Your people have strayed from where they were in their knowledge of You, their love for You, and in their relationship with You in olden times. Because of their fallen state (sin), Your creation also fell (lands, oceans, nature, creatures and the order of all things – authority, dominion, truth, righteousness, etc.). Man worship created things – false gods, themselves, and demons.

My God put things back in order. Make all things new again. Strip away the layers from man; break down the walls man has built; destroy the lies and deceptions and bring them back to the Truth (Jesus) so they can be set free of all yokes and bondages and once more come into a right relationship (divine order) with You; they can once more worship You in Spirit and Truth; then all of creation will come into order. All the glory will come back to You, my God. All the glory must come back to You my God! It is Yours my God. Take it back, take it back."

After Petra's interpretation of the Holy Spirit prayer, we realized why I was commanding "order" as I prayed. I told Petra, "Now I know why every time I am fighting evil spirits, I am always saying, 'out of order' to them." Ruth and I were as much in awe as Petra about the interpretation of The Holy Spirit's prayer. This was our first experience of a prayer being interpreted. We both knew that what Petra told us was true. Ruth is used to the way I usually pray to God. We pray together, almost daily.

Were you prepared to hear about the

prayer I described above? Well, make no mistake, The Holy Spirit chose to reveal this prayer to you to let you know that God will be taking back His glory. He will be placing His universe back into Divine order, according to His perfect design. He will not be accepting the disorder of mankind.

There is one last Holy Spirit prayer to share with you. This one is beyond awesome. The Holy Spirit was asking God to save and sanctify His people. God will not just go about changing the DNA of His people, spiritually, unless they are willing to be changed. The process is that The Holy Spirit would convict the people to freely repent of their sins and give their lives to the Lord. God will then forgive them, save them, and then begin to sanctify them.

This next prayer demonstrates how deep God can go to save His people. It was also interpreted by Petra. It took place while still on the Norwegian cruise and about two days after the first one. Again, Petra, Ruth, and I met in our cabin to pray. Ruth remembered a dream in which Petra had asked her to pray for the Indians in Guyana. She had written it down and found the note in her prayer book, which she took on the cruise. Yesterday, Petra had literally asked Ruth to pray for the people of Guyana, and today she found her recorded dream in which the same request was made by Petra.

Before praying, God had me use Ruth's anointed oil on my eyes, ears, mouth, head, and navel. Ruth and Petra also anointed themselves.

Petra first prayed for her children and family. She took authority over their situations, as we supported her in prayer. Both Ruth and Petra prayed at length for the safety of the ship, captain, crew, and passengers.

After Petra was finished, Ruth took over. She prayed for the Indians originating from the country of Guyana. During her prayer, she asked God to change their DNA which has generational curses. The moment Ruth mentioned the word "DNA" it triggered a response in my spirit. I suddenly exclaimed loudly, The Holy Spirit took over, and then started to pray in tongues (language I did not understand).

My belly was moving up and down as I prayed. Again, Petra was able to interpret The

Holy Spirit's prayer and to see what was going on, in the spirit. She said it was as if the Holy Spirit took the word "DNA" and went deeper in prayer for the Indian people in Guyana. Here is what Petra understood of the prayer.

"Father, before the Cross, when there was great wickedness on the earth, You would destroy entire nations to wipe out the wickedness. Men, women, everyone, down to the seed (children) were wiped out to ensure the wickedness was removed.

But my God, since the Cross, You do a new and different thing. You gave man skills to operate on the body. They can go into the body and remove sicknesses and diseases from the heart and different organs and parts of the body. But You my God, You are the master Surgeon, the Great

Physician of Your people! You no longer need to destroy the people to cleanse the earth of wickedness, but You can operate on the DNA of Your people. You can do surgery with the greatest precision and detail on this smallest molecule of Your people, to remove the wickedness and evil of a thousand generation, spiritually."

In the above prayer, The Holy Spirit of God prayed to Himself to surgically remove contaminated DNA from the Indians from Guyana. Wow! Are you now wishing that you were an Indian from Guyana? God has His plan to clean them up, in a unique way. Of course, it is to turn them around to serve Him alone.

The two Holy Spirit-interpreted prayer experience I had on the Norwegian cruise brought alive my expectation that God hears and answers prayers, as well as participates in the prayers of His children; those who allow Him to do so. It encouraged me to continue praying and to be confident that God not only hears and answers my prayers, but also prays for what I do not know to pray about.

The interpretations of The Holy Spirit's prayers, through me, only confirm what E.M. Bounds stated about prayer causing earth to change, causing revolution on earth, and causing God to shape policies (Bounds, 1920); as seen by Petra of God putting back the pieces of earth together and surgically changing the DNA of Indians from Guyana, through prayers.

With these awesome prayer times we had

on the Norwegian cruise, I have to wonder if God's enemy saw it and was mad. The month after our cruise ended, January 2018, we heard on the news that the Norwegian cruise ship encountered a historic storm at sea, while on their next cruise.

I believe it was the prayers of Ruth and Petra while we were on the previous cruise that kept the Norwegian ship from sinking, during the fierce storm. God knew why He had them praying at length for the safety of the ship, captain, crew, and passengers. He knew what the ship would face in the near future.

God doesn't always avert the storm, but He takes you through it. God does not move on the earth without the prayers of His children because He has given them authority and dominion on earth, once they are born again. Without the prayers from Ruth and Petra, He could not have saved the Norwegian ship. The lesson here for others is that we must be obedient to the leading of the Holy Spirit, even when we do not understand what He is doing, or where He is leading us.

I shared with you, a couple of Holy Spirit-filled prayer experiences, in addition to that for Amazon, so that all – companies, world leaders, and individuals come to understand that God – our Creator, is worthy to be praised, worthy to be glorified, worthy to be worshiped, and worthy to be acknowledged in all things and at all times.

God is taking note of our behaviors towards Him and each other. He will not tolerate disorder forever. He will put back His creation in Divine order, as it was meant to be.

I Need More Help

The quest to fulfill my assignment to write and publish book did not end with The Holy Spirit praying for Amazon. I was less than half way on my journey to accomplish this.

Amazon was not the only company God allowed me to get help from in establishing His business. There are others for which I am grateful. However, Amazon is the one on which The Holy Spirit requested me to focus my writing, due to the special role they play in His business.

There is the story of a renowned book editing company which I hired to edit the book manuscript I considered most crucial in telling my stories – *God's Mission: Spiritual Battles And Revelation of Anti-666*. In an interview with the editing manager, I told him I had some experiences with God which are equivalent to those written about in the Bible. He mentioned that the Bible is a special book, so it seemed that he did not think there could be any stories in current days which could match up to Biblical stories. From the feedback I got from the editor assigned to me, I was able to apply them to laying out the contents of the other manuscripts.

When my manuscripts were ready for

sample print, The Holy Spirit led me to a bookstore which had just started providing "books-on-demand" printing service to authors. The Holy Spirit placed a very strong desire in my spirit to get Christian workout videos to do my exercises. I went online and checked out Christian workout videos. I found one at a bookstore, close to my workplace, and decided to visit the store after work.

As soon as I entered the bookstore, I saw the "books-on-demand" printing service sign. I knew immediately that this was why The Holy Spirit wanted me to go and get a Christian workout video. I did not hesitate in signing up for this service.

A few print trials helped me to determine

which way the printing was going. It was a struggle for me since I had never done anything close to book interior, or book cover work. Other than using Word document, which I was familiar with, I had to learn two other publishing software.

If I was doing this book writing and publishing project for myself, I would have just used a publishing company to do it for me. However, I continuously reminded myself that "things would fall apart" for God's plan, if I did not publish the books the way He was directing me; that is, to establish a self-publishing company. If I should use a publishing company, they would most likely want to alter my true stories, which are also God's stories.

Help from the "print-on-demand" book

service at the bookstore was what gave me a boost in confidence with what I was doing. Indeed, God provided their help for my book writing and publishing assignment.

This Is It. Really?

Yes I got help and God prayed for Amazon. But, is this where it ends? Is there a need for more help and more prayers? After a while, I started to think that it is good I am able to have face-to-face contact with the people printing God's books; maybe, I could just do "print-on-demand" with this bookstore and limit my books to their circulation. Is this God's plan for His books? It would be less complicated for me, but is this what

He wanted?

I soon realized that I needed more help than what the "print-on-demand" service was offering. My sample prints showed that I did not have a good handle on doing book interior and cover formatting. I stopped doing the sample printing and doubled down on learning how to format book interior and cover pages. I retrieved the book publishing information I previously gathered from CreateSpace and elsewhere.

It took me some time, but in the end, I generated manuscripts with good looking book interiors and covers, when viewed in .pdf format. All the covers I created were done under the guidance of The Holy Spirit. I had to do all of them. Even though I tried getting help with the book

This Is It. Really?

covers, the help always fell through. After doing a lot of work on the book covers and contents, I felt that I was ready to go back to the bookstore and do sample prints, using their "print-on-demand" service.

Redirected to Victory

Armed with my three manuscripts, I marched into the bookstore to do my sample prints. What sample prints? To my great dismay, the "print-on-demand" service was no longer offered. Oh my God! What a disappointment. I was forced to go to another printing service provider.

I went back to the printing company which distributes books to brick and motor stores. However, God hindered me from uploading my titles. I kept getting errors. I left it alone and decided to go back to CreateSpace – the Amazon's subsidiary, which did "print-on-demand" service.

The online process of completing my sign up, loading up and previewing my manuscripts and book covers was easy to follow. However, all of this was new to me. For the few times I needed reassurance that I was on the right track, I requested help call backs and got confirmation on what I was doing, or direction as to what to do next. The preview tool that CreateSpace had was a God-send. It only took me two print samples to decide that I was done. In April 2018, I was able to publish God's three books, simultaneously.

God got the victory – hallelujah!!! He got the victory by my persistence in obeying the leading of His Holy Spirit, regardless of whatever I faced throughout the manuscript writing and book publishing process. It was The Holy Spirit Who led me to His selected printing partner. The lesson here is that we must all, as Christians, be persistent for God. We do not always have to understand everything God is telling us to do, but we must trust and obey Him.

God did not allow me to launch His books in the United States, nor did He allow me to advertise them there. He only allowed me to tell a small amount of people about them. I call them His books, because I had given them to Him. He sent me to the community in which I grew up to launch His books, at His chosen church, and by His chosen pastor.

At this point, I have to honor my cousin, Pastor Valda Bennett, for her obedience to God. I must also acknowledge her persistence in carrying out His works, even when faced with multiple challenges. I rarely come across this level of obedience to God, among His children. When God asked her to do His book launch for Him, she did not hesitate.

When I visited Jamaica in 2018, I told Pastor Bennett that I had written three books. She immediately offered to have a book launch at her church. She said another cousin of ours had recently done a successful book launch there. I told her thanks, but I would have to think about it. I knew that she was extremely busy in the community. She is constantly being called on to help with activities in the community and to pray for the sick, in addition to pastoring her church. I was wondering, "Why would she want to take on more work?" At that time, I did not realize that The Holy Spirit had asked her to do the book launch.

After I returned to the United States, I mentioned to my sister, Ruth, that Pastor Bennett offered to host a book launch in Jamaica, for me. She agreed with me that she was already too busy and shouldn't be taking on extra work. I dismissed the idea of having a book launch in Jamaica.

The next Sunday when I was having church service, The Holy Spirit led me to sing hymn # 168 from my Presbyterian Hymnal, "Ye servants of God, your Master" (The Church

Hymnary, revised edition, p.55). I started to sing verse 1, "Ye servants of God, your Master proclaim, And publish abroad His wonderful Name." As soon as I sang the words, "And publish abroad His wonderful Name," The Holy Spirit took over and I started to speak in tongues. I immediately realized that God had just confirmed that I should allow Pastor Bennett to do His book launch in Jamaica. After all, the books were His, so it was His decision to make.

Shortly after the "publish abroad" song spiritual incident, I called Pastor Bennett and told her God had confirmed that I should do a book launch in Jamaica. We discussed possible launch dates. I next turned to my book printing partner CreateSpace (Amazon) and ordered the books to be shipped directly to Pastor Bennett.

The books order went through without issues. However, Pastor Bennett had issues with the shipping company. The books were sent in multiple shipments and they did not all arrive at the same time. There was a lot of back-and-forth with the shipping company and customs. It was very tiresome for her.

Despite the many challenges, Pastor Bennett did not give up. She was determined to complete the work of God, as she had promised Him. We recognized that God was testing both of us. The test to both of us from God was, "Will you carry out my work despite all the difficulties involved? Will you remain faithful to Me, against all odds?" We did not let God down. We prayed, communicated issues and progress with each other, and did all we could until all the books were safely in Pastor Bennett's hands.

The cost to me for getting the books to Pastor Bennett was extremely high. I knew I would not even come close to recuperating what I spent by selling the books. However, I knew it was well worth what God wanted to accomplish by launching His books in Jamaica.

Shortly, after I got the good news from Pastor Bennett that all the books were safely with her, The Holy Spirit suddenly reminded me of a shipping company that specializes in shipping to Jamaica. I called them up and checked on the possible cost of shipping books to Jamaica. Based on what I was told, it would have been tremendously cheaper and almost hassle-free if I had the books shipped to me and then I shipped them to Pastor Bennett, using that shipping company.

Getting the books to Jamaica was truly a test from God. Otherwise, He would not have informed me of the easier and cheaper alternative, immediately after Pastor Bennett and I passed His test of obedience to Him and perseverance against all odds, on His behalf.

Before sending me back to my roots to launch His books, God hinted about the cost of the books and that they were treasured by Him.

Before The Holy Spirit had asked Pastor Bennett to launch God's books at her church, He had led me to attend the 58th Annual New York

International Antiquarian Book Fair, March 8-11, 2018, at Park Avenue Armory in Manhattan, New York. At the point where I did the final edits for God's books, a postcard came in the mail with the book fair invitation. This was the very first time I saw an invitation for this kind of book fair. As soon as I saw the invitation, I knew I should attend. I knew it was confirmation from God to move forward to the publishing stage, with the final edits of His books.

I went to the book fair in obedience to The Holy Spirit, not knowing what to expect. After browsing through all the stalls, I was not sure why The Holy Spirit wanted me to be there. I went away puzzled. To me, the prices of the exhibits were outrageous. They were special writings and old valuable books. They were considered to be treasured items. The lowest price I saw was $256 USD; most book prices were in the thousands of dollars (USD); I even saw one priced at $100,000 USD.

After seeing the way God continues to take pieces of the stories I wrote and fulfill them, in His own way, I came to the conclusion that the books I had written for Him were indeed special writings and were treasured by Him. He used the Antiquarian Book Fair to point this out to me.

It was only after I obeyed the leading of The Holy Spirit to launch God's books in Jamaica, I realized that there was another reason He wanted me to attend the special book fair. The prices of the books in Jamaica had to be in the low thousands, due to the foreign exchange rate. Therefore, I had to see books with prices in the thousands of dollars.

God has unusual ways of communicating with His children and providing guidance; you just have to be in tune with His Holy Spirit to recognize when and how He is communicating with you. He will use businesses, such as the one which put on the Antiquarian Book Fair, in the process of executing His works, without them being aware of it.

Pastor Bennett took on the task of advertising the book launch in Jamaica, using flyers and word-of-mouth. When she called and said that The Holy Spirit told her to have a "Town Cry" (a vehicle driving through the community while announcing an event), I mentioned to her that the same song that God used to let me know that I should do a book launch in Jamaica, has in verse 3, the words, "Let all cry aloud, and honour the Son" (The Church Hymnary, revised edition, p.55). The words were confirmation that The Holy Spirit gave her this direction. God was deeply involved in His book launch activities. I did a recording of the song from my hymnal and sent it to Pastor Bennett to use in the "Town Cry" advertisement.

God's book launch in Jamaica went very well. I had never visited Pastor Bennett's church before. When I entered, I had a wonderful surprise. The colors of the decor on the inside matched exactly the colors of the dress and shoes

I wore to God's book launch. This was just His way of confirming our obedience to Him and to let us know that He was with us; He had His book launch all planned out. We, as His children, just have to obey His directions. Pastor Bennett made the same observation with her church's décor and my matching outfit.

Pastor Bennett and I were happy to honor God with our obedience. We know that He deserves so much more than we are capable of giving. This means that as His children, we should always, always, always obey Him whenever He asks anything of us. In obedience, I wrote books for God and I have testimonies of Him executing the stories I have written. I have observed enough to write a book about "God reading His books and executing His words."

Based on the works I see God doing that are related to the books I have written; I pause at times and try to image Him reading His books and then working on what He has read. An outstanding example is the chapter I wrote in the book, *God Has Gone Corporate*, which I entitled, *Spiritual Disruption: Unleashing The Next Wave of Saving Souls.* This simply means that in order to save souls, God will enter the marketplace and disrupt it, spiritually. The chapter was written, under the direction of The Holy Spirit, to parallel what James McQuivey wrote in his book, *Digital Disruption: Unleashing the Next Wave of Innovation*.

James' book is a must read for companies.

It got God's attention. In his book, James addressed the digital trend he saw that would disrupt the marketplace. His job is to spot business trends and advise companies to get onboard and change the way they think about innovation.

God's plan is to inject Himself into the marketplace and get the attention of people, so that they can change the way they think about Him, get on board with Him, recognize Him for Who He is, and give Him the glory and praises He deserves. After all, He is the God of ALL CREATION.

A Leader's Prayer for Change, in a Time of Crisis

We are in the year 2020 when all across the world the marketplace and people's lives are disrupted – spiritually, physically, and economically. Were we prepared for this? I don't think so. Spiritually, more people are seeking God to help them get through the current pandemic. Physically, people are getting sick and some businesses and institutions are closed. Economically, closing businesses has negative consequences on people's finances; the stock market is losing money in multiple investments while a few proper. People are asked to stay at home and practice social distancing.

To put it very mildly, there is uncertainty and confusion everywhere. It is clear that people, businesses, institutions, and governments need the help of God.

Are enough people seeking the help of God – their Creator, in this current pandemic? I am hearing that, "We will get through this together. We are fighting a battle which we can band together and overcome."

In this battle, we are fighting an invisible

enemy; we do not know who will survive. This virus does not discriminate as to who to take out.

Our focus should be to make sure it is well with our souls. We should repent of our sins and turn to God – our Creator, through Jesus Christ, in order to be saved. The prayers of The Holy Spirit of God which I shared with you speak volumes as to what God expects of us. Despite what we are thinking, we cannot save ourselves.

When you are on the battlefield, you need the right kind of weapon to overcome the enemy; you need the right help to overcome the enemy; you need God – our Creator. He has power over EVERYTHING. For too long, people have been disregarding God – thinking that they do not need Him; they can take care of everything themselves;

A Leader's Prayer for Change, in a Time of Crisis

and they have all kinds of technologies that give them power. Let us rethink the need for God in every aspect of our lives.

World leaders everywhere need to be conscious of the "God of ALL CREATION." He needs to get the respect due to Him, knowing that we are living in a world created by Him, knowing that everything we create uses His raw materials, and knowing that we are TOTALLY dependent on Him. As such, world leaders need to pray to the ALMIGTHTY God for the protection of their nations, while sincerely repenting of the nation's sins.

Right now, the MIGHTY hand of God is stretch across the entire world, as each nation battle the current pandemic. Leaders of nations should look at the example of the Prime Minister of Jamaica (Andrew Holness) who openly prayed at Jamaica's National Day of Prayer in March, 2020. He repented of the nation's sins, asked God forgiveness of their sins; asked God for mercy, and reminded God of the powerful covenant He has with the country of Jamaica, in the form of The Jamaica National Anthem. He also blended the Jamaica National Pledge in his prayer (Prime Minister of Jamaica Andrew Holness, 2020).

I was extremely impressed by the powerful prayer of Prime Minister Holness on behalf of Jamaica, but even more impressed was God Himself. He inspired me to write about this prayer and He was not satisfied that I gave an overview of the prayer. He wanted me to write it out in its entirety so that other nations can see what kind of prayer is required from them to move His hand, on their behalf.

Before getting into prayer, Prime Minister Holness mentioned that he knows it is always symbolic when the leader says to the people of the nation, "Let us pray." He declared his heart has been moved to support the National Day of Prayer. He recognized that the nation's own efforts would never be good enough. He recognized that there is a force that is stronger than us. He said, "*Even the mightiest of warriors, in the midst of war, hoping for victory, turned to heaven and asked for God to let the sun stand still so that they can win over the evil forces.*"

Prime Minister Holness' prayer started

with worship and exaltation of God. *"Eternal God, and Father, we worship and exalt Your name. You are God above all gods, governments, institutions, the church, and above all of us. And now, oh God, according to Your will and purpose, I come into agreement with all prayers which have been prayed; and ask that You grant them, in Jesus' name. Eternal Father, throughout our history, many have wronged us – our loved ones and our nation, from time to time. We forgive them all and give these matters into Your hands today."*

Prime Minister Holness continued, *"I come to You today on behalf of my nation, my family, my wife is here with me, in prayer; and every family, and every person in Jamaica. I come as Prime Minister of Jamaica on behalf of myself and all*

A Leader's Prayer for Change, in a Time of Crisis

leaders of the state, their various administrations, staffs, operational arms, and their various agents and agencies. Lord, God, and Eternal Father, I come, acknowledging that we have sinned against the people of Jamaica. We have sinned against our fellowman. We have sinned against our family members and relatives. We have sinned against our neighbors, strangers, and visitors. We have sinned against the children, the youth, and the unborn. We have sinned against the poor and the weak and the elderly and the sick. We have sinned against the free and the imprisoned. We have sinned against those in the care of the state, including the children, the mentally ill, the prisoners, and others. We repent, oh God of all our sins committed against these and all persons – local and international, in the name of Jesus Christ of Nazareth.

I come on behalf of all the political leaders – government and oppositions. I come on behalf of the parliament of Jamaica – all the cabinet members, all the senators, the legislators, all members of the judiciary and penal system and members of the security forces. I come on behalf of all institutions, individuals, and groups throughout Jamaica, representing the civil governance system, along with their administration, managers, staffs, and fellows.

I come acknowledging that we have sinned against you. We have sinned against our people and we repent. We ask for forgiveness, mercy, and cleansing, in Jesus' name. Hear our prayer and forgive us of all sins, in Jesus' name.

A Leader's Prayer for Change, in a Time of Crisis

Lord, I come to You on behalf of every Jamaican, here in Half Way Tree square, every Jamaican throughout the island, and every Jamaican in the diasporas. We hereby seek your face and turn from our wicked ways, asking for Your mercies and forgiveness for our sins and seek, by faith and by choice, to humble ourselves in Your sight, acknowledging our sins individually and collectively. We now take responsibility for our sins as we come to You. Grant us grace to obey You, in Jesus' name.

We also acknowledge, as described in the words of Daniel, the prophet, oh Lord, the great and dreadful God, keeping the covenant and mercy to them that love You and to them that keep Your commandments; we have sinned and have committed iniquity and have done wickedly and have rebelled, even by departing from Thy precepts and from Thy judgments; neither have we hearkened unto Thy servants, the prophets, which spake in Thy name to our kings, our princes, and our fathers, and to all the people of the land.

To the Lord our God belongs mercies and forgiveness; though we have rebelled against Him, neither have we obeyed the voice of the Lord, our God, to walk in His laws, which He set before us, Thy servant, the prophet.

Oh my God, incline Thy ear and hear, open Thine eyes and behold our desolation and the city which is called by Thy name; for we do not present our supplications before Thee for our righteousness, but for Thy great mercies. Oh Lord, hear; oh Lord, hearken and do; differ not for Thine own sake, oh my God, for the city and the people are called by Thy name.

Teach us Thy way and lead us into Thy paths. Give us sight and direction, teach us true respect for all and give us a heart that fears You and regards the sanctity of life. Heavenly Father, it is our deep desire for our nation to be released from the burden of the sins of our past and to be reconciled to Almighty God.

Have mercy and grant us our request, grant us national healing and restoration, and transformation, and reformation, as only You can, in Jesus' name. Keep us free from evil powers, be our light through countless hours.

We decree and declare that Jamaica, under

God, shall increase in beauty, fellowship, and prosperity, and play her part in advancing the welfare of the whole human race. Grant us these mercies and blessings, in the name of Jesus Christ of Nazareth. Amen" (Prime Minister of Jamaica Andrew Holness, 2020).

The Question of Social Change

We know that we are in a crisis situation with this current pandemic. More individuals and some world leaders have been seeking God for help. I am not at all surprised that the world is in this economic and health crisis. I am seeing this as a time of spiritual disruption. The book of Revelation is worthwhile reading to get more insights into this end-time event, and more to come.

It is not just individuals who need to turn to God. As spiritual disruption is taking place across the world, companies need to recognize that even in business, God is needed. God wants to get their attention too. After all, He owns EVERYTHING; and EVERYONE needs to know that.

In 2019, God gave me a question to ask at a company's town hall meeting. The question is, "How do you prepare for social change – the unexpected one that impacts your business?" I thought I would be asking this question to the CIEO of the company, but it was asked of one of the chairmen of the board of directors of the company. I later had the opportunity to tell him

The Question of Social Changes

that the question I asked was a prophetic one, which God gave me. I briefly explained that I was highly connected to God and that He will reveal things to those who serve Him.

The question which God gave me to ask the chairman of the board of a large, multi-national company is relevant to what is happening to the world with the current pandemic. We are certainly experiencing social changes – unexpected ones; ones for which we were not prepared.

The next question is, "Are companies, world leaders, church leaders, and everyone looking to God to take them through this? This virus is not only taking lives, but impacting the world's economy. Are we paying attention to God, now that He is dealing with us in the area where our attentions are mostly focused – the economy?

The company to which God directed His unexpected social change question has been profiting tremendously because of the social change brought about by the current pandemic – changes so life altering that I could not have imagined such a prophetic outcome. I now realize that the question was related to the upcoming increased profitability of the company. I hope the chairman remembers the question God asked of him, through me.

I am saying that God asked the "unexpected social change" question, through me because of the way the question came about. In 2019, before Good Friday, my neighbor invited me to her church for a special Remembrance Service for Jesus Christ, in the evening. She offered to give me a ride. That evening, I was running about 20 minutes late, so when I did not see her car in her driveway, I decided to go to the church to which I thought she belonged. I went to a Seventh Day Adventist church nearby. There were a few people rehearsing. A man told me that the presentation was the next day and that I should come back at 9:00 a.m.

The next morning when I checked with my neighbor to travel with her, she said that the event was yesterday. She did not see my car, so she thought I was not home. I told her I went to the Seventh Day Adventist church when she did not come to give me a ride. She told me that was not her church; hers is the Kingdom Hall of Jehovah Witness.

Since I was already dressed to go, I went to the event at the Seventh Day Adventist church. They were having Sunday School and not the Remembrance Service as I expected. I asked someone and she told me that the service would be after Sunday School. They were having discussions from a book by Claudio and Pamela Consuegra. The lesson was, "Preparing for Change." The following are excerpts which led to the social change question:

"Life is full of changes. Things change all the time...Often, changes come unexpectedly. We are going along in a routine when, suddenly, instantly, everything changes, and we are caught completely

off guard. On the other hand, sometimes we can see changes coming. We are given forewarnings, signs, and indicators that let us know things are going to be different. When this happens, it's wise to start preparing, to whatever degree possible, for what we can see coming. Many of these changes are big..." (Claudio Consuegra, Pamela Consuegra, 2019).

After group discussion of the reading, each group leader presented a different topic about change. One group leader said that although it was not in the book, he was adding "social changes." After the presentations about change, there was baptism, followed by a service of song, music, and poetry – all centered around the great story of the sacrifice Jesus Christ made by dying for our sins.

Later when I met two of my classmates at a restaurant to have lunch. I explained why I was late, they surprised me by saying that while they were waiting for me, they were discussing changes in the church and society. With this confirmation, I knew that God wanted me to ask about social changes in the upcoming townhall meeting I was going to attend, at my job. He had given me the material, at the Seventh Day Adventist church, to formulate the question.

Before I went to the townhall meeting to ask the question about social change, my coworker shared a dream he had about me, which was similar to one he had previously about a priest and fire burning in the church. In that dream, there was something he had to do before he could get holy water from the priest. In the dream about me, there was fire burning inside a building and I was at a podium. I had a book reading and my coworker came to me. When he was within reach, I touched his forehead with something in my hand.

I know that at times, dreams of fire meant the move of The Holy Spirit. My coworker said he looked up the meaning of dream about priest and the meaning he got was "change coming." This was yet another confirmation that I should ask a question about "change."

At the townhall meeting, when the chairman of the board was introduced, I learnt that he had worked at a company for which I had

The Question of Social Changes

also worked. He was also from the country from which my hiring manager at that company originated. Before asking the prophetic question about unexpected social change, I had to introduce myself. The Holy Spirit moved me to include my connections to the chairman, through my previous employer and my hiring manager there.

I can relate the connections I have with the chairman to my coworker's dream about a priest in which he had to be qualified for the holy water. After the townhall ended, the chairman came from the podium and spoke to me about the previous employer we had in common. He was curious as to when I left and the location I worked.

Like my coworker having to be qualified to

get the holy water from the priest, in his dream, I had to be qualified for the chairman to come and speak to me. I was able to tell him that the question I had asked him was a prophetic one given to me by God; that I was highly connected to God, so he could use me in that way.

I am sharing the experience I had which led me to the "unexpected change" question, so that the reader can better understand the works of God through individuals and through corporations.

I have many other stories about the move of God in the company which got the unexpected social change question. To write about them, would produce a book, similar to this size. God is working in many places, yet people do not recognize His works; unless He reveals His works to them.

You have to be in tuned to God to be able to recognize His works and His guidance in your live. God uses spiritual incidents, which connects things, or circumstances together to form a solution. Some people might think of what they encounter as coincident, but when you can clearly see the works of God in the situation, you know it is not coincident, but spiritual incident. Spiritual incidents do happen in businesses.

I shared the social change question which God directed to a company, to emphasize that I have seen the works of God in other businesses, not just Amazon. However, His request is that the main focus of my writing be on His works with His business partner - Amazon.

Get Noticed

I hope that the experiences I shared with you about the works of God in the way He selected His business partner and establish His product – books, will give you better insights into Who our Creator is. His works often go unnoticed. He is now seeking to "get noticed." In doing so, He needs business partners. God has unusual ways of selecting His business partners. Do you know if you have a God-selected company?

Why did God choose Amazon as His book printing partner? It could be for reasons I don't know of. What is obvious to me is that Amazon had the best setup to help authors doing self-publishing. I realized this at the end of searching out other printing companies. However, I see where Amazon started out selling books before moving into other areas of business. The business I have established for God also started out selling books; in this case, books only about His works. I don't know if there are any other parallels with Amazon and God's business, but who knows.

The writing of this book was inspired by The Holy Spirit and requested by Him to be released in the height of the current pandemic, which at the time of this writing, is moving across the world. God wants the attention of all businesses, all world leaders, and all individuals.

Seeing that God – our Creator, has allowed a disruption of the world's economy, will you turn to Him, repent of your sins, ask forgiveness of your sins, and establish a close relationship with Him? I pray that God will allow all to see the need for Him in their lives and in all that they do.

Bibliography

Bounds, E.M. *E.M. Bounds on PRAYER*. Whitaker House, 1920.

Claudio Consuegra, Pamela Consuegra. Family Seasons: Adult Sabbath School Bible Study Guide, 2019.

McQuivey, James. *Digital Disruption: Unleashing the Next Wave of Innovation.* Amazon Publishing, 2013.

Prime Minister of Jamaica Andrew Holness. WhatsApp, 2020.

Prince, Derek. *The Gifts of the Spirit: Understanding and Receiving God's Supernatural Power in Your Life*. Whitaker House, 2007.

The Church Hymnary, revised edition. London Oxford University Press. Glasgow, Melbourne, 1927

The Holy Bible. King James Version. Holman Bible Publishers, 1979.

About the Author

Jenness Reid is a child of God who He has been using to fight spiritual battles. Her relationship with God is such that He can use her at His highest level of spiritual warfare.

    Jenness has been publishing books about her experiences with The Trinity – God, Jesus Christ of Nazareth, and God's Holy Spirit.

Books By This Author

God Works Through Dreams

This book has a wide variety of natural and spiritual dreams and their fulfillment, which is useful in interpreting dreams. It will spark interest in the significance of dreams. Readers will appreciate the power of dreams, as God uses dreams to deliver messages. They will realize that the enemy of their souls uses dreams to work against people.

Dreaming is a part of life. God created us with an aptitude for dreams. Do you know the value of your dreams? Are your dreams warnings, revelations, or directions from God; are they from

Satan, or, are they to be ignored?

This book will spark a curiosity in you about your own dreams as the author shares her journey of how she learned to understand her dreams. This book reflects the beginning of the author's spiritual journey. God started the journey with dreams. She shares her dream stories so that others might realize that God works through dreams, not only in biblical days, but also in present time. Her stories include experiences of spiritual afflictions through dreams, created by those who practice spiritual wickedness.

You may not be close enough to God right now. But, do you know if He has a plan for you – that has been shown to you through dreams, which you may be ignoring? This book will leave you asking the question, "Should I be paying attention to my dream?" According to biblical prophecy, God will be pouring out His Spirit on everyone; your children will prophesy; old men will dream dreams; and young men will see visions (Joel 2:28-29). This book provides insights into such a day, as prophesied by the prophet, Joel.

God's Mission: Spiritual Battles And Revelations Of Anti-666

Spiritual warfare might be scary to some people. It involves fighting and overcoming evil and demonic forces sent against you by someone skilled in satanic crafts. Sometimes, it is Satan challenging you in the anointing God placed on your life. When faced with spiritual warfare, ready or not, you must deal with it.

The reality of spiritual warfare comes alive in this book, as the author relates her experiences. God gave her and her family dreams to prepare them for her experiences. She can now help others fight their spiritual battles, overcome forces of darkness, and reject the Biblical "mark of the beast."

It might seem strange for someone to speak of being attacked by evil and demonic spirits. You will most likely be labeled as being crazy, if you dare to share your experiences. However, if you only take the time to search the Bible, you will find many stories of Jesus casting out evil and demonic spirits from people who were sickened in one way or the other by them. Even Jesus' disciples were able to cast them out in Jesus' name after He gave them the power to do so.

It was a sad day for earth when Satan and his

angels were cast out of Heaven. Adam and Eve were the first to fall into Satan's trap. Satan and his angels are the powers by which people inflict injuries on others, spiritually. The Bible tells of people working curious arts (satanic crafts), which were documented in books (Acts 19:19); so, it continues in our days. People skilled in satanic crafts are inflicting injuries on others, through spiritual means.

The author is a victim of such spiritual wickedness. This book is about God taking her through His mission of battling evil and demonic spirits and conquering them. She has been through experiences of outright spiritual battles with the Trinity (God, Jesus, and the Holy Spirit) providing help throughout her ordeals. She was exposed to different levels of evil spirits and demons and had the revelation of how to handle the

Biblical "mark of the beast" – 666.

God Has Gone Corporate

The author shares her experiences of God directing every aspect of establishing a business for Him. The awesomeness of God – The Creator, has often been overlooked, or, dismissed. The many experiences with God, which the author shares, cannot be readily dismissed. Saving souls is now at the business level where people are focused.

This story of God's business is unique. The reader will come to realize that God has commissioned the author to establish a business for Him so that He will get the attention of all people, across the world. Everywhere people are caught up in economic gains, or struggling to survive economic crisis. In such atmosphere, God is often taken out of the picture.

This book tells stories of how God directed the author to go into business for Him, with the Trinity [God (Adonai), Jesus Christ (Yeshua HaMashiach), and the Holy Spirit (Ruach HaKodesh)] as Directors. It sets the tone for God's corporate image so that secular corporations will come to understand "Who" has entered the marketplace. In the Bible, references to God's business point to managing the affairs of the church, which includes sharing God's words, bringing souls to God, and taking care of the poor and needy.

The new, radical approach God has to enhance the works of the church is to enter the corporate world in such a way that businesses and consumers have to pay attention to Him, as He disrupts all that have been disrupted – showing that He is God of ALL things.

www.ingramcontent.com/pod-product-compliance
Lightning Source LLC
Chambersburg PA
CBHW031424290426
44110CB00011B/517

9 780983 199984